Real Side Hustles That Work

Practical Ways to Make Extra income Without Quitting Your 9-to-5 Job

By Dane Kane

Copyright © 2024 by Diana Kane
All rights reserved. No part of this publication may be reproduced, stored or transmitted in any form or by any means, electronic, mechanical, photocopying, recording, scanning, or otherwise without written permission from the publisher. It is illegal to copy this book, post it to a website, or distribute it by any other means without permission.

Diana Kane asserts the moral right to be identified as the author of this work.

Table Of Contents

Introduction 1

Chapter 1: Unlocking New Income Opportunities 6

Chapter 2: How a Side Hustle Can Transform Your Life .. 12

Chapter 3: Discovering Your Profitable Passion 17

Chapter 4: Building a Thriving Side Business 23

Chapter 5: Staying Ahead of the Game 30

Chapter 6: Selecting a Profitable Side Hustle 36

Chapter 7: Types of Side Hustles You Can Start Today ... 42

Chapter 8: YouTube as a Side Hustle 48

Chapter 9: Video Editing for Clients 56

Chapter 10: Pet Services - Dog Walking and Pet Sitting . 59

How to Start 60

Chapter 11: Tutoring and Teaching Online 62

Chapter 12: Creating and Selling Online Courses 66

Chapter 13: Starting a Blog 72

Chapter 14: Selling Ebooks on Kindle Direct Publishing (KDP) 79

Conclusion 86

Real Side Hustles That Work

Introduction

In today's fast-paced world, side hustles have become more than just a passing trend; they represent a powerful way to secure your financial future, learn new skills, and even uncover passions you never imagined. Whether you're looking to boost your income, chase a dream, or take charge of your financial destiny, side hustles offer the flexibility and opportunities to make it all possible.

Why Side Hustles Matter?

So, what exactly is a side hustle? At its core, it's any job or business you pursue in addition to your primary source of income. It could range from freelancing, running an online business, to sharing a skill you're passionate about. The beauty of a side hustle lies in its adaptability—it works around your existing commitments while empowering you to reach both your personal and financial goals.

But why should you consider starting one?

The Benefits of Extra Income

An extra stream of income from a side hustle can drastically improve your financial situation. It might just be the key to moving from living paycheck to p

aycheck to achieving true financial freedom. Whether it's paying off debt, saving for a trip, or simply creating a financial cushion for the unexpected, side hustles give you the power to build a more stable future.

Beyond the financial perks, side hustles offer a sense of accomplishment and pride as you watch your efforts pay off in real time. They provide a deeper sense of purpose, reminding you that you're in control of your own future.

Moreover, side hustles let you tap into talents and passions that your day job may not allow. It's your chance to try new things, refine your skills, and grow in ways you hadn't expected. Who knows, your side hustle could even evolve into a full-time career.

How Will This Book Help You?

This book is your step-by-step guide to discovering, starting, and growing a side hustle that fits your unique life. From identifying the right hustle based on your skills and interests, to offering practical strategies for managing your time effectively, each chapter is designed to equip you with actionable advice to ensure your success.

If you've been curious about adding another stream of income but haven't known where to start—or perhaps you've tried before but faced setbacks—you're in the right place. I'm here to help you take that first step and turn your side hustle idea into a thriving reality. With a clear, step-by-step approach, we'll address everything you need to know to create a side hustle that not only works but thrives.

By the end of this book, you'll have the knowledge, tools, and confidence to start and scale a side hustle that aligns with your goals and lifestyle. It's time to stop dreaming and start doing—because the future you are working for is waiting.

How to Use This Book

To truly benefit from *Real Side Hustles That Work*, approach it with focus and dedication. This isn't just a collection of ideas—this is a practical, hands-on guide that will walk you through each step of your side hustle journey.

Follow the Step-by-Step Process

Each chapter is designed to build upon the previous one, leading you through a structured process.

Whether you're just brainstorming side hustle ideas or already taking action, following the chapters in sequence will help you stay on track and make consistent progress. You'll learn about the best side hustle options for your strengths, then develop strategies for long-term success. The key is to focus on one step at a time without rushing ahead.

Take Action After Every Chapter

Reading is important, but it's an action that will bring your side hustle to life. After each chapter, take immediate action—complete the exercises, brainstorm your ideas, and put what you've learned into practice. The more actively you engage, the clearer your path will become. Small, consistent actions over time lead to big results.

Stay Consistent and Motivated

Building a side hustle is both exciting and challenging. There will be highs and lows along the way, but the key to success is consistency. Dedicate regular time to your side hustle, even if it's just a few hours a week. Remember, progress is progress—no matter how small it seems. Keep your eyes on the bigger picture and celebrate every milestone, no matter how minor. With steady effort and perseverance, your side hustle will grow into something you can truly be proud of.

By following this book as your roadmap and committing to consistent action, you'll be on your way to building a side hustle that truly works—for you. Let's dive in and start turning your goals into reality!

Chapter 1: Unlocking New Income Opportunities

Discover Your Hidden Potential

To transform your side hustle idea into a profitable venture, the first step is to uncover the untapped potential within you. This involves recognizing your unique skills and passions and learning how to turn them into income-generating opportunities. The exciting part is that you don't need to start from scratch—you already possess everything you need to get started.

Evaluate Your Skills and Passions

Take a moment to reflect on what you're good at. What do people often ask you for help with? It might seem like an obvious question, but it's essential to honestly assess your talents. Sometimes, we overlook our own skills because they come naturally to us, but that doesn't make them any less valuable.

Ask yourself these questions to begin:

- **What activities do I enjoy in my free time?**
  Perhaps it's creating artwork, organizing events, helping others learn, or fixing things around the house. These passions often make great side hustles because they don't feel like "work."
- **What do others regularly seek my help with?**
  Are you the go-to person for tech support, social media tips, or DIY advice? These are indicators that others recognize your expertise, even if you don't always see it yourself.
- **What skills do I apply in my job or hobbies?**
  If you're in customer service, you likely have strong communication skills, which could be perfect for freelance writing or coaching. If you're proficient in tools like Excel or Photoshop, your skills can be offered to businesses or individuals who need assistance.

Write down these skills and passions. Don't limit yourself to only the most obvious talents—think creatively about how your everyday interests and abilities can be turned into profitable side hustles.

Identify Opportunities Around You

Opportunities are everywhere—you just need to know where to look. The secret lies in spotting gaps, needs, or challenges in your daily life or community, then figuring out how you can provide a solution. Often, the best side hustle ideas are simple answers to problems that others might not have noticed yet.

Here's how you can identify these opportunities:

- **Look for needs within your community:** Think about the people you interact with regularly—family, friends, neighbors, or coworkers. Do any of them need help with something you excel at? Perhaps you could assist a local business with their social media, offer tutoring services to students, or help someone organize their home. Often, your first customers will be those closest to you.
- **Use online platforms to spot demand:** Websites like Reddit, Facebook groups, or local community boards are great places to find unmet needs. For instance, if you notice there's a rising demand for pet-sitting in your area and you love animals, why not offer pet care services? Platforms like Upwork, Fiverr, or Freelancer also give insight into popular services that are in demand.
- **Monitor trends and consumer behavior:** Keeping an eye on emerging trends can help you spot opportunities you hadn't thought of. If you notice a growing interest in home

workouts, and fitness is your passion, you might want to create workout guides or even offer online coaching. The key is staying observant and being ready to offer value where it's needed.

Once you've spotted a need, brainstorm ways to use your existing skills and passions to address it. You don't need all the details figured out yet, but this is the foundation that will drive you forward.

Leverage What You Already Know

Now that you've identified your skills and potential opportunities, it's time to leverage what you already have to build your side hustle. The beauty of a successful side hustle is that it doesn't require reinventing the wheel—it's about utilizing your current resources, knowledge, and mindset to take action.

Mindset for Success

Before you dive into your side hustle, it's important to adopt the right mindset. The journey you're about to embark on will take focus, determination, and a willingness to overcome challenges. But remember, success doesn't happen overnight, and that's perfectly fine.

The first step is believing in your own abilities. Acknowledge that your skills are valuable and that you have what it takes to succeed. The more confident you are in your abilities, the more likely others will be to pay for your services or products.

It's also important to be realistic about the time and effort required. Balancing a side hustle with a full-time job or other commitments calls for dedication, but with the right mindset, you'll view this as an exciting challenge, not an obstacle.

Embrace a Growth Mindset

A growth mindset is essential for your side hustle success. It means embracing challenges, learning from setbacks, and being open to constant improvement. When you approach your hustle with this mindset, you'll see mistakes as valuable lessons that help you become better at what you do.

For example, if your first freelance project doesn't go as planned, instead of quitting, you'll look for ways to improve. Maybe you'll refine your communication, adjust your pricing, or better understand your client's needs. Each step, even the setbacks, is a chance to grow and become stronger.

A growth mindset allows you to see learning opportunities in every situation—even the most difficult ones. Hold onto this mindset, and you'll keep evolving your hustle into something more successful with each passing day.

Stay Open to New Possibilities

Your side hustle journey may not always follow a straight path. You might start by offering one service only to realize that there's a better opportunity that suits your skills or interests. The key to long-term success is staying open to new possibilities and adapting as you go.

For example, you might launch a cooking blog, but over time, you notice your readers are more interested in meal planning. If you're open to this feedback and willing to pivot, you could adjust your side hustle to meet this new demand by offering meal planning services or creating a digital cookbook.

Flexibility and adaptability are essential in building a successful side hustle. The more open you are to change, the more likely you are to uncover fresh opportunities and find lasting success.

By focusing on what you already know, adopting the right mindset, and staying open to new possibilities, you can unlock hidden potential and begin building a side hustle that aligns with your skills, passions, and goals. It's time to take action and start your journey toward earning extra income.

Chapter 2: How a Side Hustle Can Transform Your Life

A side hustle isn't just a way to earn extra income – it's an opportunity to reshape your life in ways that go far beyond your financial situation. Whether your goal is to achieve financial independence, personal growth, or a blend of both, a side hustle has the potential to help you accomplish things you never thought possible. Let's explore how it can change your life.

Unlock Financial Freedom

For most people, the primary motivation behind starting a side hustle is to improve their finances. A side hustle can pave the way to financial freedom – the ability to manage your money, reduce stress about bills, and make decisions that align with your personal aspirations.

Pay Off Debt Faster

Debt can often feel like a burden weighing you down, whether it's student loans, credit card bills, or a car loan. A side hustle offers a chance to pay off that debt more quickly, lightening the load on your finances. By directing the extra income you earn from your side hustle toward your debts, you can make a noticeable impact on what you owe. Even small contributions can accumulate over time, and the more you pay off, the less you'll have to worry about monthly bills, freeing up money for other priorities.

Imagine the relief of no longer being tied to debt. With steady effort, your side hustle could bring you closer to this reality faster than you might think.

Save for Your Big Dreams

Whether you're working toward buying a house, traveling the world, or saving for your child's education, reaching big goals requires big savings. A side hustle offers you the chance to save more than your regular income allows, bringing those dreams closer to reality. By setting specific savings goals, you can allocate a portion of your side hustle earnings to fund your future ambitions.

Think about the dreams you've always had but thought might take years to accomplish. A side hustle could help speed up the process. Rather than relying solely on your regular salary, you now have an additional income stream to bring those dreams into reach.

Build a Financial Safety Net

Life is unpredictable – emergencies can arise at any time, from medical bills to car repairs or even unexpected job loss. That's why building an emergency fund is crucial. A side hustle gives you the opportunity to create a financial cushion to safeguard against life's uncertainties. Even if you start with small contributions, over time, this fund will provide the security you need to handle unexpected situations without resorting to credit cards or loans.

With a side hustle, you can build your emergency fund more quickly, giving you peace of mind and greater financial stability.

Personal Growth Beyond Finances

In addition to the financial benefits, a side hustle can foster significant personal growth. As you work on your side business, you'll learn new skills, gain independence, and develop a sense of confidence that you may not have experienced before. These personal growth aspects can be just as valuable – if not more – than the money you make.

Acquire New Skills

Starting a side hustle is about more than just earning money – it's about expanding your skill set. Whether it's learning how to market your business, design websites, or manage finances, running a side hustle pushes you to develop new abilities.

For instance, if you launch a freelance writing business, you'll gain experience in writing, research, time management, and possibly even SEO (search engine optimization). If you sell handmade jewelry, you'll learn about e-commerce, product photography, and customer service. These skills not only benefit your side hustle but also enhance your main career, making you more versatile and valuable in the job market.

A side hustle encourages continuous learning. It provides the opportunity to try new things, step outside your comfort zone, and develop professionally, all while expanding your capabilities.

Gain Independence and Confidence

One of the most rewarding aspects of a side hustle is the sense of independence it provides. By building something of your own, you gain control over your work, your schedule, and your income. This autonomy can be incredibly empowering.

As you grow your side hustle, you'll also notice your confidence soar. Each achievement – from landing your first client to hitting your income target – will boost your belief in your abilities. Over time, you'll realize you're capable of accomplishing more than you ever imagined.

A side hustle not only helps you become financially independent but also mentally and emotionally resilient. You'll find yourself becoming more self-reliant, adaptable, and confident in facing challenges and succeeding.

The Big Picture

A side hustle has the power to change your life in profound ways. Financially, it can help you pay off debt, save for big dreams, and build a financial safety net. Personally, it encourages you to learn new skills, gain independence, and grow in confidence. Most importantly, a side hustle empowers you to take control of your future, both financially and personally. It's not just about the money – it's about the transformation that comes with it.

So, take the leap. Embrace the life-changing potential a side hustle can bring and watch your life evolve in ways you've always dreamed of.

Chapter 3: Discovering Your Profitable Passion

The Journey of Self-Discovery

To find a side hustle that resonates with your passion and allows you to earn income, the first step is self-discovery. It's about identifying what excites you and exploring how that enthusiasm can be turned into something profitable. This journey begins with a few key questions to help you reflect on what truly drives you:

What Brings You Joy?

While this may seem like a basic question, it's vital to your success. The activities that bring you happiness, spark your creativity, or make time fly by are often the gateway to a profitable side hustle. Passion is a powerful motivator, making your work feel less like a task and more like an enjoyable pursuit.

Think about how you spend your free time. What do you find yourself gravitating toward? Whether it's photography, writing, gaming, crafting, or organizing, these hobbies are more than just leisure activities – they could be the foundation for a profitable side hustle. Ask yourself:

- What activity do I look forward to the most?

- What could I do for hours without feeling bored?

The answers to these questions could point you toward a side hustle that not only fits your lifestyle but also keeps you motivated to succeed.

What Problems Can You Address?

Once you've identified what you love to do, the next step is to figure out how you can solve problems with your passion. A successful side hustle isn't just about doing what you love – it's about addressing the needs of others. There are countless challenges people face every day, and if you can find a way to offer a solution, you've unlocked a potentially profitable opportunity.

Consider the everyday problems that people struggle with. Can you help them with organizing their space? Could you design workout plans to help people get in shape? Are you an expert in a certain field, such as career advice, finance, or tech, and able to offer guidance to others?

By understanding the problems people face and aligning them with your skills and passions, you can create a side hustle that is both valuable to others and financially rewarding for you.

Turning Your Passion Into Profit

Once you've pinpointed your passions and identified how they can address real problems, the next step is to figure out how to monetize them. There are several ways to turn what you love into a source of income, and the options are more accessible than you might think.

Earning From Your Hobbies and Skills

One of the easiest ways to start earning money from your passion is by monetizing your hobbies and skills. If you already love doing something, why not get paid for it?

Here are a few practical examples:

- **Photography**: If you're passionate about photography, you can monetize it by offering services such as portraits, event photography, or even selling stock photos online. Platforms like Shutterstock and Adobe Stock provide opportunities for photographers to sell their work.

- **Writing**: If writing is your passion, explore freelance writing or content creation.

Platforms like Upwork, Fiverr, and ProBlogger are great for connecting with clients looking for writing services. You can also start your own blog and earn through ads or affiliate marketing.

- **Crafting or Art**: If you love crafting or creating art, consider selling your creations on platforms like Etsy or at local craft fairs. From handmade jewelry to paintings to home décor, there's always a demand for unique, handcrafted items.

The beauty of monetizing your hobbies is that it doesn't require huge upfront costs. You can begin with what you already know and offer it to people who value it.

Combining Skills for Unique Offerings

To stand out in a competitive market, consider combining multiple skills into one unique service. This allows you to create something distinctive that appeals to a specific audience, often leading to higher-paying opportunities.

For instance, if you have skills in both graphic design and social media marketing, you could offer services that combine both. You might create eye-catching social media posts and help businesses manage their accounts. If you're skilled in both fitness and nutrition, you could offer personalized coaching packages that address both exercise and meal planning.

Another example could involve combining your love for writing with personal development. You could offer coaching services alongside custom journals or self-help content.

The key is to think creatively about how to combine your skills into a package that stands out in the market. By offering something specialized, you're more likely to attract a targeted audience that values your expertise and is willing to pay for it.

Putting It All Together

Finding your profitable passion is all about aligning what you love with what others need. The more you can merge your interests and skills with real-world problems, the more successful your side hustle will be.

Keep in mind that turning passion into profit doesn't happen overnight. It takes patience, persistence, and a willingness to adapt and learn along the way. But by identifying your passions, recognizing the problems around you, and thinking outside the box about how to monetize your skills, you'll be on the path to creating a side hustle that not only brings in extra income but also brings fulfillment.

So, take the time to reflect on what excites you, identify the needs of those around you, and explore how you can monetize those passions. With creativity and action, your passion can become a profitable reality.

Chapter 4: Building a Thriving Side Business

Turning your side hustle into a full-fledged business is about more than just generating extra income – it requires a strategic approach, focus, and persistence. The great news is that you don't have to jump in all at once. You can take it step by step, starting small and growing as you go. Let's explore how to build a side business that brings in income while providing personal satisfaction.

Start Small, Dream Big

When beginning your side business, it's essential to start with what you have rather than waiting for the "perfect" circumstances. You don't need a big budget or a massive team to get moving – many successful ventures started as small, side projects with little investment.

Leverage What You Have

Take stock of the skills, knowledge, and resources already available to you. For example, if you're offering a service, you likely have access to a computer, internet, and the necessary expertise. If you're selling products, you might already have raw materials or can find them affordably. Starting where you are with the tools at your disposal is a smart approach.

Resourcefulness is a hallmark of successful entrepreneurs. Utilize free or low-cost tools like social media to get the word out about your business. Don't overlook the power of word-of-mouth and personal networks to secure your first clients or customers. Focus on gaining momentum instead of perfection.

Set Practical Expectations

While it's easy to get excited about the potential of your new side business, it's important to set practical expectations. It's unlikely that your side business will instantly replace your full-time income, so be prepared for gradual growth.

Remember, success isn't instant. Rather than expecting overnight fame or riches, aim for small, attainable goals that will keep you motivated. For instance, you could set a goal to acquire your first 10 clients or sell 50 units of your product within the next few months. These milestones will offer a sense of achievement and maintain your energy. As you build momentum, your business will naturally expand.

Key Steps to Success

While every business is unique, there are a few key steps you can take to set a solid foundation for long-term success.

Define Clear Goals

The first step in building a successful side business is clarifying what success looks like to you. Having a clear vision will guide your path forward. Start by setting clear, achievable goals for your business. These goals should be specific, measurable, and broken down into actionable steps.

For example, a measurable goal could be: "I want to earn $500 a month from freelance writing by the end of six months." This allows you to track your progress and adjust your approach as necessary.

You may want to break your goals down into smaller tasks, such as "I'll reach out to 5 potential clients this week," or "I'll complete 2 projects this month." These smaller, immediate actions will help you stay focused on what's in front of you, all while working toward your broader goal.

Create a Simple Business Plan

You don't need a complicated business plan. At its core, a business plan is simply a blueprint for how you'll operate and grow your business. A well-thought-out plan helps you focus your energy and stay on track.

Start by answering a few key questions in your business plan:

- **What product or service am I offering?**
  Be clear about what you're providing, whether it's freelance writing, digital marketing, or handmade goods.

- **Who is my target audience?**
  Identify who will benefit from what you offer. Are you targeting individuals, small businesses, or larger corporations? Knowing your ideal customers will help you craft marketing strategies that speak directly to their needs.

- **What is my unique selling proposition (USP)?**
  Determine what sets your business apart from competitors. Whether it's your expertise, pricing, or exceptional customer service, knowing your unique value will help attract clients and customers.

- **How will I market my business?**
  Outline the methods you'll use to promote your business, such as social media, networking, or even paid advertising.

Having a clear marketing strategy will ensure you stay focused on building awareness for your business.

Answering these questions will give you a clear direction, guiding your decisions and actions as you move forward.

Market Your Business Effectively

Even if you have an outstanding product or service, it won't matter if no one knows about it. Marketing is the key to connecting your business with potential customers. The good news is that you don't need a huge budget to start marketing effectively.

Here are some strategies to help you build your brand:

Maximize Social Media

Platforms like Instagram, Facebook, LinkedIn, and Twitter are free and powerful tools to market your business. Use these platforms to share valuable content, engage with your audience, and promote your products or services. Once your business grows, you can explore paid ads.

Network Actively

Networking is a great way to spread the word about your business. Attend industry events, join online forums, and connect with other entrepreneurs. These relationships can help you find new clients, customers, and potential business partnerships.

Referral Programs

Word-of-mouth marketing is incredibly effective. Encourage satisfied customers to refer their friends or colleagues to your business. You can offer them incentives such as discounts, freebies, or other rewards for each new customer they bring in. This is an excellent, low-cost way to grow your customer base.

Create Valuable Content

Creating valuable content is another way to attract potential clients. Whether it's through blogs, tutorials, videos, or podcasts, content marketing helps establish your authority in your field. Providing useful, relevant information builds trust and attracts an audience who sees you as a valuable resource.

The key to effective marketing is consistency. Building your brand and customer base takes time, so don't expect immediate results. Focus on consistently engaging with your audience, nurturing relationships, and offering valuable content. The more consistent you are, the more visible your business will become.

Final Thoughts

Building a successful side business doesn't require a massive investment or complicated strategies. Start with what you have, set realistic goals, and create a simple business plan to guide your growth. Focus on consistent marketing efforts to build your brand and customer base. By following these steps, you'll create a solid foundation for your side business, and over time, you'll transform your hustle into a thriving business. Take it one step at a time, and with determination, you'll achieve your entrepreneurial dreams.

Chapter 5: Staying Ahead of the Game

Building a successful side hustle or business isn't just about working hard—it's about working smart. Staying ahead means managing your time effectively, protecting your energy, and balancing the demands of your side hustle with the other aspects of your life. The secret to staying productive and moving your side hustle forward is using the right strategies, staying organized, and avoiding burnout. Let's dive into how you can stay ahead, keep progressing, and do it all without sacrificing your well-being.

Productivity Hacks

When you're balancing a side hustle with a full-time job, family, and personal life, it's easy to feel overwhelmed. But with the right productivity strategies, you can maximize your time and achieve more with less stress.

Mastering Time Management

Time is one of the most precious resources you have, and how you use it can make or break your side hustle. The good news is, with the right time management techniques, you can make steady progress without feeling like you're falling behind.

One highly effective time management strategy is the Pomodoro Technique. This involves working in short, focused intervals (usually 25 minutes) followed by a 5-minute break. After four cycles, take a longer break of 15-30 minutes. This approach helps you stay sharp and focused while preventing fatigue, especially when working on your side hustle after a full day at your main job.

Another great tip is to time block your day. Dedicate specific time slots to work on your side hustle and treat them as appointments you can't cancel. For instance, commit to working on your business from 7:00 PM to 8:30 PM every weekday. Time blocking keeps you disciplined and ensures you make consistent progress—even if it's just a small step forward.

Utilizing Productivity Tools

In today's digital age, a variety of tools are available to help you stay organized, track progress, and boost your productivity. Here are some tools that can streamline your side hustle:

- Trello or Asana: These project management tools are perfect for organizing tasks, setting deadlines, and collaborating if needed. They help ensure no task slips through the cracks.

- Google Calendar: This simple tool can help you schedule your work time, as well as personal and family activities. Set reminders to stay on top of your side hustle tasks.

- Notion: An all-in-one workspace to track goals, manage projects, and keep notes on ideas. Notion is great for keeping everything in one place, from business plans to brainstorming sessions.

- Focus@Will: If you struggle to concentrate, this service provides scientifically optimized music that enhances focus and productivity. It's a great companion for working on your side hustle.

Using these tools helps you stay organized, reduce mental clutter, and make the most of the time you have available.

Balancing Work and Life

While productivity hacks are essential, it's just as important to maintain a healthy balance between your side hustle and personal life. Without this balance, the demands of your side hustle can lead to stress, burnout, and strained relationships.

Staying ahead isn't just about working hard—it's about protecting your well-being.

Preventing Burnout

Burnout occurs when you push yourself too hard without taking adequate time to rest and recharge. The good news is burnout can be prevented. By proactively managing your energy, you can maintain a steady, sustainable pace for your side hustle.

A key to avoiding burnout is recognizing your limits. Don't try to do everything all at once. Set realistic goals and don't be too hard on yourself if things don't go perfectly. Break large tasks into smaller, manageable steps, and give yourself permission to take breaks when necessary.

Taking regular breaks is crucial. Even if your side hustle feels like an endless task, stepping away for a day or even a few hours can give your mind the reset it needs. Whether it's a walk outside, a short vacation, or a weekend off, taking time away will give you fresh energy and a clear mind to keep moving forward.

Setting Boundaries and Schedules

One of the best ways to balance life and work is to create clear boundaries between your side hustle and personal time. When you work from home or run a side business, it's easy for the two worlds to blend together, leading to stress and frustration. Set clear boundaries to maintain your peace of mind.

Start by defining specific hours for your side hustle and stick to them. Treat this time as a commitment, but also know when to switch off. For example, if you've set aside 7:00 PM to 9:00 PM to work on your business, honor that time, and once it's over, focus on family, relaxation, or hobbies.

Communicate your boundaries to those around you—family, friends, and roommates should know when you're working and when you need downtime. This will help everyone respect your schedule and minimize distractions.

Also, make sure you set boundaries for yourself. Avoid working late into the night or sacrificing your weekends to catch up. Work within your limits and take regular breaks. Balance is key—if you focus only on your business, you risk burning out. If you neglect your business, you won't make progress. Finding the right balance benefits both your personal life and your business.

The Takeaway

Staying ahead of the game requires intentionality with how you manage your time and energy.

Productivity strategies like time blocking and using productivity tools help you stay on track and maximize the limited time you have. But it's just as important to create a balance between your side hustle and personal life. Prevent burnout by setting realistic goals, taking breaks, and respecting your boundaries. By working smart and maintaining balance, you'll ensure long-term success without compromising your well-being.

Chapter 6: Selecting a Profitable Side Hustle

Choosing the right side hustle is one of the most critical steps you'll take in your entrepreneurial journey. While there are countless opportunities available, not all of them will lead to sustainable success. To build a profitable and long-lasting side hustle, it's important to assess potential ideas carefully. This chapter will walk you through evaluating business opportunities based on key criteria that will help ensure you're on the path to long-term success.

Evaluating Potential Side Hustles

Before diving into any business, it's essential to assess it against several key factors. This helps ensure you're choosing a side hustle that matches your skills, fits your schedule, and aligns with your goals. Let's break down the key aspects to consider:

Low-Investment Ventures

You don't need a hefty financial investment to start a successful side hustle. Many businesses get off the ground with minimal upfront costs, relying more on your expertise, creativity, and hard work. When evaluating side hustles, look for opportunities that require little to no initial investment. The beauty of low-investment businesses is that they're often easier to scale, as you can reinvest profits into growing your operations.

Think about the skills or resources you already have. Do you possess a particular talent or knowledge that could serve as the foundation for a business? Can you offer a service with minimal overhead or inventory? Starting with what you already possess minimizes financial risk and lets you see a return on your time faster.

High-Demand Offerings

A side hustle's profitability often depends on the demand for the service or product you're offering. It's crucial to select a business that solves a real problem or meets an ongoing need. A service with high demand means you'll have no shortage of potential customers, making it easier to generate consistent income.

When choosing your side hustle, ask yourself whether the service you're offering is something people need or want regularly. High-demand services typically have an established market, ensuring a steady stream of customers. It's not just about riding the latest trend—it's about offering something with lasting value that people are willing to pay for.

Key Criteria for Success

Once you have a shortlist of potential side hustle ideas, it's time to evaluate each one through three critical lenses: profitability, time commitment, and scalability. These factors will help you determine if a side hustle is sustainable and aligns with your personal objectives.

Profitability Potential

The primary goal of a side hustle is to generate additional income, but not all side hustles offer the same earning potential. To evaluate the profitability of your idea, consider the following:

- Revenue Streams: How will your business make money? Are there multiple income sources, or will you rely on just one? A side hustle with diverse revenue streams—like products, services, or passive income—tends to be more robust and profitable over time.

- Pricing Strategy: What will you charge for your products or services? Conduct market research to see what others are charging and determine if your pricing structure will allow you to meet your financial goals. Be mindful that pricing too low can limit profits, while pricing too high could reduce demand.

- Operating Costs: Even businesses with low startup costs have ongoing expenses, such as marketing, software tools, or materials. Make sure you account for these costs to ensure your side hustle remains profitable after factoring in your expenses.

Time Commitment

Time is one of your most valuable resources when building a side hustle. To avoid overwhelming yourself, assess how much time you can realistically dedicate to your business without disrupting your other commitments. Keep the following in mind:

- Available Hours: How many hours per week can you invest in your side hustle? Make sure you have enough time to stay consistent and make progress. It's essential to pick a side hustle that aligns with your available time.

- Time vs. Reward: Consider the relationship between the time you put in and the money you earn. Some businesses may take time to generate a return (for example, product creation or customer acquisition). Ensure the time commitment aligns with your financial goals and lifestyle.

- Work-Life Balance: Your side hustle should not come at the cost of your health or personal life. Balance is key. While your side hustle will require time, it should fit into your existing schedule without sacrificing family time, health, or well-being.

Scalability

Scalability refers to the ability to expand your business without a proportional increase in time and effort. A scalable business allows you to grow your profits without needing to invest significantly more time or resources. When assessing scalability, consider:

- **Automation and Delegation:** Can you automate tasks or delegate responsibilities as your business grows? For example, using software to handle administrative duties or hiring part-time help can free up your time and allow you to focus on growth strategies.

- **Market Potential:** Is the market large enough to accommodate growth? A scalable side hustle has access to a broad audience, whether through new products, services, or geographical expansion.

- **Long-Term Viability:** Consider whether the business has room to evolve. Some side hustles are ideal for short-term income, while others offer long-term growth potential. Ask yourself if the business can adapt to changing trends or grow in response to your evolving goals.

Key Highlights

Choosing the right side hustle isn't just about selecting an interesting idea—it's about assessing opportunities through the lens of profitability, time commitment, and scalability. By evaluating potential business ideas based on these key factors, you can identify side hustles that not only align with your personal goals but also offer the potential for long-term success. Start by leveraging your existing skills, think about the time you can commit, and make sure there's room to grow. A side hustle that fits into your lifestyle and allows for future expansion will set you up for sustained income and personal fulfillment.

Chapter 7: Types of Side Hustles You Can Start Today

When you're ready to kickstart your side hustle, one of the first steps is figuring out which type of hustle aligns best with your skills, interests, available time, and financial objectives. This chapter provides an overview of several side hustle options you can begin right now. Although we will explore each hustle in more detail in upcoming chapters, this guide will help you pinpoint the best fit for your current situation.

Service-Based Hustles

Service-based side hustles are often the most versatile and beginner-friendly. These businesses typically don't require significant upfront costs and can be launched quickly, especially if you already have the necessary skills. Whether you're working online or in-person, service-based hustles can quickly become a reliable source of income as you grow your client base.

Freelancing

Freelancing is an excellent way to monetize your skills by offering services on a project-by-project basis. Whether you're a writer, web developer, graphic designer, or consultant, freelancing allows you to work on your terms—set your hours, choose your projects, and determine your rates. The best part? Freelancing is highly adaptable. No matter what skills you have, there's a market for them. Websites like Upwork, Fiverr, and Freelancer make it easy to connect with clients and scale your business as you gain more experience.

Tutoring

If you're knowledgeable in a specific subject, tutoring can be a fulfilling and profitable side hustle. Whether you're helping kids with math, guiding college students through complex subjects, or teaching adults new skills like coding or business management, tutoring provides a great way to share your expertise. You can find students via platforms like Tutor.com and Wyzant, making it easy to offer lessons remotely and at your convenience.

Dog Walking

For those who love animals, dog walking is a simple side hustle that requires little investment.

Pet owners often need reliable help walking their dogs during work hours or while they travel. Platforms like Rover can help connect you with clients in your area. This hustle is flexible, requires minimal startup costs (just some good walking shoes and maybe some dog-walking gear), and gives you the opportunity to spend time outdoors while getting paid.

Digital Product Hustles

Digital products are unique because you create them once and can sell them repeatedly with little extra effort. Thanks to the internet, these types of side hustles allow you to reach a global audience and generate passive income. If you have a creative streak and are comfortable with digital tools, these hustles might be perfect for you.

Selling Digital Art

If you're an artist, selling digital art is an excellent way to turn your passion into profit. You can create digital designs, illustrations, or printable artwork and sell them through platforms like Etsy, Redbubble, or Gumroad. Once you've created your digital products, there's no need to worry about inventory or shipping. You can instantly deliver your creations to customers, making it a hands-off business once it's up and running.

Print-on-Demand Products

Print-on-demand (POD) is a business model that allows you to design custom products—like t-shirts, mugs, or phone cases—and sell them online without managing inventory. Platforms like Printful, Teespring, and Redbubble handle the printing and shipping for you. Your primary focus will be designing appealing products that will attract buyers. Once your store is set up, sales are relatively passive, allowing you to focus on marketing your products and growing your brand.

Passive Income Hustles

Passive income hustles are designed to generate revenue with minimal ongoing effort. Although most passive income ideas require significant time or work upfront, they can eventually create a reliable source of income once established. These hustles are ideal for those who prefer to put in the work initially and enjoy earning money over time.

Blogging

Blogging has long been a popular method for generating passive income. By creating valuable content that attracts an audience, you can monetize your blog through ads, affiliate marketing, or sponsored posts. Blogging lets you focus on topics you're passionate about—whether it's personal development, fitness, travel, or niche interests. Once you've built an audience and your blog starts gaining traffic, you can earn money consistently through these monetization methods, making it a fantastic long-term side hustle.

YouTube

YouTube offers another lucrative platform for passive income. If you enjoy creating video content, YouTube allows you to monetize through ads, affiliate marketing, and sponsored content. As your channel grows and gains more subscribers, YouTube can become a reliable source of income. Although it takes effort and consistency to create valuable content, the potential for earnings is significant. Whether your videos are tutorials, reviews, or vlogs, you can build an engaged audience that generates passive income for years.

Affiliate Marketing

Affiliate marketing involves promoting other people's products and earning a commission on sales made through your referral links. You don't need to create a product of your own—instead, you simply share a link to someone else's product, and when someone makes a purchase, you earn a commission.

Affiliate marketing can be done through blogs, social media, or YouTube channels. Once you've set up your affiliate links, your content can continue to generate income for you without additional effort, making it an ideal passive income side hustle.

Key Highlights

- **Service-based hustles** like freelancing, tutoring, and dog walking offer low-investment, flexible options that can quickly turn into profitable ventures.

- **Digital product hustles**, including selling digital art and print-on-demand items, allow you to create products once and sell them repeatedly, minimizing effort and maximizing income.

- **Passive income hustles** such as blogging, YouTube, and affiliate marketing provide the potential for ongoing revenue with minimal ongoing effort once the initial work is done.

By choosing the right hustle based on your skills, time commitment, and goals, you can begin building a side business that fits into your lifestyle. Whether you're offering services, creating digital products, or exploring passive income options, there's a side hustle out there for everyone.

Chapter 8: YouTube as a Side Hustle

Why You Should Consider YouTube for Your Side Hustle

Starting a YouTube channel isn't just about making money—it's a chance to connect with a global audience, share your unique knowledge, and unleash your creativity. With millions of active users, YouTube offers incredible potential to build a following and turn your passion into profit. By creating engaging and consistent content, you can monetize your channel through ads, sponsorships, and affiliate marketing, all while doing something you love.

The best part? YouTube allows you to work on topics that excite you. Whether it's technology, education, entertainment, or any other area, you can create a channel that reflects your interests. While success on YouTube requires dedication and patience, the reward of building a loyal audience and earning income makes it all worthwhile.

Getting Started with YouTube

Launching your YouTube channel is a straightforward process. Here's how to get started:

1. **Create a Google Account**
   If you don't have one already, sign up for a Google account. This is essential to use YouTube and access its monetization options through Google AdSense.

2. **Set Up Your YouTube Channel**
   Once you have your Google account, follow these simple steps to create your YouTube channel:

   - Log in to YouTube and click on your profile picture in the top-right corner.

   - Select "Create a Channel."

   - Choose a name that represents your content and upload a profile picture.

   - Hit "Create Channel," and you're all set!

3. **Verify Your Phone Number**
   To access features like custom thumbnails and longer video uploads, verify your phone number. This ensures you can use the platform's full potential.

4. **Brand Your Channel**
   Your channel's branding plays a significant role in attracting viewers. Add a channel banner and video watermark to give your channel a professional appearance. These visual elements help make your channel recognizable.

5. **Complete Your "About" Section**
   This is where you introduce your channel to potential subscribers. Be clear and concise, explaining what type of content you'll be posting and what viewers can expect.

Finding Your YouTube Niche

Choosing the right niche is crucial for attracting an audience. A niche is a specific topic or area your channel will focus on. Some popular niches include:

- Gaming
- Cooking
- Technology
- Health & Fitness
- Fashion
- Finance
- Comedy

- Music
- Vlogging

The key is to pick something you're passionate about and make sure there's an audience interested in it. Don't be afraid to narrow down your niche. For example, rather than just "fitness," focus on a more specific topic like "home workouts for beginners."

Understanding Your Audience

Knowing who you're creating content for is essential to success. Define your target audience by considering factors such as age, interests, and the kind of content they consume. Understanding these elements will help you tailor your videos to meet their needs, whether it's educational, entertaining, or both.

Crafting Your Value Proposition

Your value proposition is the promise you make to your viewers. It's what sets you apart and answers the question, "Why should people watch my videos?" For instance, if you're making tech tutorials, your value proposition might be: "Simplifying the latest tech for beginners."

Analyzing Your Competitors

Looking at other channels in your niche can offer valuable insights into what works. Study your competitors to understand their most popular topics, how they engage with their audience, and which types of videos get the most views. This can help you fine-tune your content strategy and find ways to differentiate your channel.

Generating Video Ideas

Don't run out of content! Here are a few ways to brainstorm video ideas:

- Look for trending topics within your niche.

- Think about common questions your audience might ask.

- Use tools like YouTube's search bar or Google Trends for inspiration.

- Watch videos from competitors for new ideas.

And remember, you don't have to be an expert. You can create content based on your learning journey or share your experiences. For example, I recently saw a video titled "Day 1 of Coding," where the creator simply shared their first steps in learning to code. It's proof that there's potential for content in everything you do, and you can create videos about your everyday experiences.

Using Keyword Research to Optimize Your Videos

Before uploading your videos, make sure to conduct keyword research. Keywords are the terms people search for on YouTube, and using them in your video titles, descriptions, and tags can help your videos get discovered. Tools like Google Trends or the YouTube search bar can help you find the best keywords for your content.

Getting the Right Equipment

While you don't need to invest in high-end gear right away, having the right equipment will improve your video quality. Start with your smartphone, which can record great video, and use free or affordable editing software. As your channel grows, consider upgrading your equipment with:

- A higher-quality camera
- An external microphone for clearer sound
- Lighting to enhance video quality
- A tripod for stability

But don't stress over having the perfect setup at the start—focus on making great content that resonates with your audience.

Uploading Your First Video

Once you've created your first video, it's time to upload it. Simply click the camera icon at the top of YouTube, select "Upload Video," and follow the instructions. Remember to optimize your video's title, description, and tags with relevant keywords so it can be easily found.

Bonus Tips for YouTube Success

1. **Understand YouTube's Algorithm**:
   YouTube rewards content that encourages engagement. Videos with more likes, comments, and shares are more likely to be recommended by the algorithm. Focus on creating content that prompts viewers to interact.

2. **Experiment with Different Content Formats:**
   Try out various formats like YouTube Shorts, live streams, or regular uploads to see what works best for your audience and to keep things fresh.

3. **Be Consistent:**
   Consistency is key. Upload videos regularly, whether that's weekly or bi-weekly, and stick to your schedule. This helps build momentum and keeps your audience engaged.

With these steps, you're now ready to start your YouTube side hustle. Success on YouTube won't happen overnight, but with consistency, dedication, and a focus on creating valuable content, you can build a successful and profitable channel. Stay committed, and remember, every video is a step toward turning your passion into a thriving side hustle

.

Chapter 9: Video Editing for Clients

Why Video Editing?

The demand for video editing has skyrocketed in recent years, fueled by the rise of online content creation. With platforms like YouTube, Instagram, and TikTok thriving, content creators, influencers, and businesses are in constant need of polished, professional videos. This opens up a fantastic opportunity for freelance video editors to step in and offer their services.

Benefits of Video Editing as a Side Hustle

- High Demand from Creators: As digital media continues to dominate, content creators and businesses are always searching for talented editors who can enhance their content.

- Flexibility: Video editing is a versatile remote job that can be done from anywhere with a computer and an internet connection.

- Creative Freedom: You'll have the chance to use your creativity to transform raw footage into engaging, compelling content.

Getting Started

1. **Learn the Basics:**
   Begin by mastering the fundamentals of video editing, such as cutting clips, adding transitions, and syncing audio. It's important to familiarize yourself with industry terms like resolution, aspect ratio, and frame rate.

2. **Choose Your Editing Software:**
   While advanced software can be expensive, there are plenty of free and affordable tools to help you get started:

- **Free Options:** DaVinci Resolve (robust and feature-packed), HitFilm Express (ideal for beginners)

- **Paid Options:** Adobe Premiere Pro (the industry standard), Final Cut Pro (excellent for Mac users)

3. **Learn from Free Resources:**
   Take advantage of free tutorials and courses online. Channels like Justin Odisho on YouTube offer beginner-friendly, step-by-step guides on popular editing techniques.

These resources are invaluable in helping you build your editing skills.

4. **Create a Portfolio:**
   Even without paying clients, you can build a portfolio by editing sample videos—these could be mock trailers, short videos, or even documenting your editing journey with a "Day 1 of Learning Video Editing" video. This demonstrates your progress and creativity.
5. **Offer Your Services:**
   Start by offering your video editing services on platforms like Upwork, Fiverr, or Freelancer. You can also reach out directly to content creators, local businesses, or acquaintances who might need help with their video projects.
6. **Keep Evolving:**
   The world of video editing is fast-paced, with new tools and trends emerging constantly. Stay ahead by watching tutorials, participating in online editing communities, and experimenting with creative projects to refine your skills.

By honing your video editing expertise, you can create a profitable side hustle that allows for both creative expression and the flexibility to work remotely.

Chapter 10: Pet Services – Dog Walking and Pet Sitting

Why It Works

The demand for pet services, such as dog walking and pet sitting, has risen as more people adopt pets and juggle busy schedules. Pet owners want the best care for their furry companions, and this provides a steady need for dependable pet caretakers.

Benefits of Pet Services

- **Flexible Hours:** You have the freedom to choose your own schedule, deciding how many clients to take on.

- **Steady Local Demand:** Pet care is an ongoing need, making this an evergreen side hustle.

- **Low Start-Up Costs:** The main investment is your time, along with basic supplies like leashes, treats, and a love for animals.

- **Emotional Rewards:** Spending time with pets is fulfilling and therapeutic, offering joy and connection.

How to Start

1. **Advertise Locally:**
   Start by distributing flyers in local areas such as pet stores, veterinary clinics, and community boards. Utilize local social media groups to spread the word and offer discounts to first-time clients to build trust and garner reviews.

2. **Leverage Pet Service Apps:**
   Sign up on platforms like Rover, Wag!, and Care.com, which connect pet owners with reliable walkers and sitters. Fill out your profile with a friendly photo, any relevant certifications, and testimonials from previous clients to stand out.

3. **Build Your Reputation:**
   Ensure you provide excellent service by being punctual, responsible, and attentive to the pets' needs. Keep pet owners updated with pictures and messages during walks or while pets are in your care. Ask happy clients to leave reviews or refer you to others.

4. **Optional Certification:**
   To further boost your credibility, consider earning certifications in pet first aid or dog training. Joining a pet care association is also a great way to connect with others in the field and learn from experienced professionals.

5. **Set Competitive Rates:**
   Research local rates for dog walking and pet sitting services. Offer package deals for daily walks, weekend sittings, or long-term pet care. Consider introducing loyalty programs or seasonal discounts.

By providing reliable, loving pet care, you can grow a dedicated client base and enjoy the benefits of spending time with animals while making extra income.

Chapter 11: Tutoring and Teaching Online

Online tutoring has surged in popularity, driven by the growing demand for personalized learning and the convenience of remote work. This side hustle offers flexibility, control over your rates, and the satisfaction of helping others achieve their educational goals.

Who Can Tutor?

Online tutoring is an excellent opportunity for individuals with knowledge in a subject or skill they are passionate about teaching. While formal teaching experience isn't always required, solid expertise and communication skills are essential for success.

Types of Tutors

- **Academic Subjects:** Help students with subjects like math, science, or history.

- **Language Learning:** Teach languages such as English, Spanish, or Mandarin to non-native speakers.

- **Specialized Skills:** Offer lessons in music, coding, digital marketing, or career coaching.

Where to Tutor

1. **VIPKid:**
   Specializes in teaching English to students in China. Requires a bachelor's degree and teaching experience. Tutors are paid per class, with bonuses for excellent performance.

2. **Preply:**
   A platform that connects tutors with students around the world for subjects like languages, academics, and business. Tutors set their own rates and schedules.

3. **Chegg Tutors:**
   Focuses on academic tutoring, offering a wide range of subjects. Tutors are paid hourly and can earn bonuses based on positive reviews.

4. **Wyzant:**
   This US-based platform connects tutors with local and online students. Tutors can set their own hourly rates and work directly with clients.

How to Get Started?

1. **Choose Your Niche:**
   Focus on a subject or skill that you excel at and enjoy teaching. Research what's in demand and where your expertise fits.

2. **Create a Professional Profile:**
   Write a compelling bio that highlights your qualifications, experience, and teaching style. If possible, include a friendly photo and a video introduction.

3. **Set Competitive Rates:**
   Research the going rates for tutors in your subject area. Starting with slightly lower rates can help you build a reputation, allowing you to gradually increase your rates.

4. **Build Your Reputation:**
   Provide engaging and personalized lessons that cater to your students' needs. Be patient, encouraging, and adaptable, and always deliver high-quality lessons. Request reviews from satisfied clients to strengthen your profile.

5. **Stay Consistent and Keep Learning:**
   Maintain a regular tutoring schedule and continue improving your skills by taking courses or learning new teaching methods.

Many successful tutors build their own teaching materials, such as worksheets or video lessons, and create personal brands through social media or YouTube to attract more clients.

Tutoring can be a rewarding way to share your knowledge and make extra income. With dedication and the right platform, it can transform into a sustainable and fulfilling side hustle.

Chapter 12: Creating and Selling Online Courses

Creating and selling online courses is one of the most powerful side hustles available today. With the rapid growth of e-learning platforms, turning your expertise into a course allows you to not only help others develop new skills but also create a steady stream of passive income.

Why Are Online Courses A Great Side Hustle?

High Income Potential:

Once your course is created, it can be sold repeatedly with minimal ongoing effort. This means you can earn income around the clock, even while you're sleeping, thanks to the scalability of online courses. With the right marketing strategies, a single course can generate significant passive income over time.

Global Reach:

Your course can reach learners all over the world, expanding your audience and creating opportunities for more sales. This global accessibility increases the potential for success.

Flexible Teaching Format:

You have the freedom to design your course however you want. Whether you prefer video lectures, live webinars, or downloadable materials, you can create a learning experience that suits your strengths and schedule.

Evergreen Content:

Courses that teach skills in areas such as web development, digital marketing, or graphic design remain valuable over time. With occasional updates, these evergreen courses can continue to generate revenue for years to come.

How to Get Started: A Step-by-Step Guide

1. Select a Profitable Course Topic

Start by identifying your area of expertise. This could be anything from a professional skill to a personal hobby. Once you've decided, research the demand for your topic on platforms like Udemy, Coursera, or LinkedIn Learning. Focus on solving specific problems that potential students are actively searching for.

2. Set Clear Learning Goals

Organize your course into modules and lessons, with each having clear, actionable objectives. This will help learners track their progress and stay motivated.

3. Create High-Quality Content

- **Script Your Lessons:** Write detailed scripts for each lesson to stay focused and ensure clarity.

- **Record Video Lessons:** Use good lighting, a quality microphone, and a clean backdrop. If you're camera-shy, consider using screen recordings or voiceovers.

- **Incorporate Visual Aids:** Make learning easier with slides, graphics, and animations.

- **Add Quizzes and Assignments:** Keep students engaged and reinforce key concepts with interactive elements.

4. Price Your Course

Consider offering a free introductory module to attract an audience and build trust. If your course has multiple levels, use tiered pricing to cater to different needs and budgets.

Course Hosting Platforms: Where to Sell Your Course

- **Udemy**:
    - Pros: Large built-in audience and marketing tools.
    - Cons: Higher platform fees and revenue sharing.
    - Best for those just starting who want a simple setup.
- **Teachable**:
    - Pros: Full control over pricing and branding.
    - Cons: Requires more effort to market the course.
    - Ideal for those aiming to build a personal brand.
- **Skillshare**:

- Pros: Subscription-based platform with a supportive community.
- Cons: Earnings depend on student engagement and watch time.
- Great for those looking for ongoing, subscription-based income.

- **Thinkific:**

  - Pros: No revenue sharing, complete customization options.
  - Cons: Steeper learning curve and higher pricing plans.
  - Best for creators who want full control and customization.

Tips for Success

- **Develop a Personal Brand:**
  Create a website and establish a strong presence on social media to effectively promote your courses.

- **Engage with Students:**
  Offer live Q&A sessions or respond to student questions regularly to build a relationship and keep learners motivated.

- **Provide Certificates:**
  Adding completion certificates can increase

the value of your course and encourage students to finish.

- **Update Your Content Regularly:** Keep your course fresh by adding new lessons or updating outdated material to reflect the latest trends.

- **Leverage Email Marketing:** Build an email list of potential students to promote new courses and updates directly to your audience.

By following these steps and focusing on delivering real value, you can transform your knowledge into a sustainable business that continues to grow. With the right approach, your online courses can provide a long-term source of passive income while helping others reach their goals.

Chapter 13: Starting a Blog

Blogging has become a cornerstone of the digital world. Whether you're looking to share your thoughts, promote a business, or create a community around your interests, blogging offers an accessible and impactful way to establish your online presence. In this chapter, I'll walk you through the process of starting a blog from scratch—covering everything from choosing the right niche to turning your blog into a source of income.

Understanding the Power of Blogging

Before we dive into the technical details, it's essential to grasp what blogging is all about and why it has become such a dominant force online. A blog is a type of website that regularly publishes posts, ranging from written articles to multimedia content like images and videos. These posts are typically displayed in reverse chronological order, with the most recent content appearing at the top.

Blogs began gaining popularity in the early 2000s through platforms like Blogger and WordPress, which made it easy for anyone to create a personal website. Over time, blogs have evolved from simple personal journals to powerful marketing tools. Today, they are not only great for expressing ideas but also for driving traffic to businesses and building an audience.

No matter if you're passionate about a specific topic or want to use blogging for business growth, it's a fantastic platform to connect with like-minded people and share your knowledge.

Choosing Your Blog's Niche

One of the most crucial decisions when starting a blog is picking a niche. This niche will define the focus of your blog, whether it's personal finance, travel, technology, health and wellness, or something more specialized like gaming or knitting.

To make the right choice, consider both your passions and the demand in the market. Research trending topics using tools like Google Trends or keyword research platforms. Your blog should aim to solve specific problems or meet the needs of your target audience.

A focused niche helps you stand out in the crowded blogosphere, attract a dedicated audience, and makes it easier to monetize in the long run.

Setting Up Your Blog

Once you've decided on your niche, it's time to set up your blog. While the technical steps might seem intimidating at first, with the right guidance, anyone can launch a blog quickly.

1. Choose a Domain Name

Your domain name is your blog's web address (URL). It's crucial to select a name that is catchy, memorable, and relevant to your niche. Keep it simple and easy to spell. For example, if your blog is about healthy living, names like "HealthyHabits.com" or "LiveWellNow.com" could work. If your desired name is already taken, consider variations or adding words that complement your theme.

Once you've picked a name, you can buy your domain through providers like GoDaddy, Namecheap, or through your hosting provider.

2. Select a Web Hosting Provider

Web hosting is what makes your blog accessible online. There are several hosting services to choose from, with popular options like Bluehost, SiteGround, and DreamHost. When selecting a provider, look for features such as:

- Easy WordPress installation
- Fast loading times
- Reliable customer support
- Strong security features

Most hosting services offer affordable plans designed for bloggers, so you won't have to worry about paying for features you don't need. After choosing a hosting plan, you'll connect your domain name to your hosting account and get your blog online.

3. Install WordPress

WordPress is the most widely used platform for blogging. It's easy to use, highly customizable, and offers a vast selection of themes and plugins. Most hosting providers offer a one-click installation for WordPress, which means you can have your blog set up within minutes.

Once WordPress is installed, you'll have access to your blog's dashboard, where you can start customizing the look, feel, and structure of your blog.

4. Pick a Theme

Your blog's design is vital for attracting and retaining visitors. WordPress offers both free and premium themes that can give your blog a professional appearance without needing advanced design skills. Choose a theme that aligns with your brand, is mobile-responsive, and features a clean, easy-to-navigate layout.

Creating Valuable Content

The key to a successful blog is engaging, high-quality content. Your content should resonate with your audience and provide them with value. Whether you're writing about personal experiences, offering advice, or sharing insights, make sure your content is both informative and entertaining.

1. Write Engaging Posts

Start by writing blog posts that align with your niche and address the needs or interests of your audience. Focus on topics that solve problems, answer questions, or inspire action. Mix up the types of content you create, including how-to guides, listicles, personal stories, and opinion pieces.

Each post should follow a clear structure: a compelling introduction, a body with in-depth information, and a conclusion that ties everything together. Use headings, subheadings, bullet points, and visuals to break up the text and make your posts more reader-friendly.

2. Optimize for SEO

Search engine optimization (SEO) is the practice of optimizing your content so it ranks higher in search engine results. By using relevant keywords, optimizing your images, and crafting SEO-friendly titles and meta descriptions, you can increase your blog's visibility.

Use tools like Google Keyword Planner or Ubersuggest to find the best keywords for your niche. Once you've identified them, incorporate these keywords naturally into your blog posts, titles, and URLs.

Monetizing Your Blog

Once your blog is up and running and you've published several posts, it's time to consider how to make money from your efforts. There are several strategies for monetizing a blog, and many bloggers combine multiple methods to maximize earnings.

1. Affiliate Marketing

Affiliate marketing is one of the most effective ways to earn money from blogging. By promoting products or services that align with your niche, you can earn a commission whenever someone makes a purchase through your affiliate link. Companies like Amazon offer affiliate programs that allow bloggers to earn money by recommending products.

2. Ad Revenue

Another way to generate income is through advertisements. Google AdSense is a popular network that places ads on your blog based on your content and your visitors' interests. You earn money each time someone clicks on an ad displayed on your site.

3. Sponsored Posts

As your blog grows, companies may approach you for sponsored posts. These are articles that promote a business's product or service, written by you in exchange for payment. These posts are typically labeled as "sponsored" to distinguish them from regular content.

Key Takeaways

Starting a blog is an exciting and accessible way to share your ideas, build a community, and even generate income. By selecting the right niche, setting up your blog, creating valuable content, and monetizing your efforts, you can turn blogging into a rewarding venture. Keep in mind, building a successful blog requires patience, consistency, and engagement with your readers. Take it one step at a time, and enjoy the process of creating something meaningful and impactful online!

Chapter 14: Selling Ebooks on Kindle Direct Publishing (KDP)

If you're passionate about writing and eager to share your knowledge, stories, or expertise, publishing an ebook through Amazon's Kindle Direct Publishing (KDP) can be an excellent way to make it happen. KDP not only offers an intuitive platform for authors, but also gives you access to Amazon's vast global marketplace, enabling you to reach readers worldwide. Whether you're a first-time author or someone looking to streamline your publishing process, this chapter will guide you through the entire journey of publishing and selling your ebook on KDP.

Why Choose KDP for Your Ebook?

Before we dive into the details of the publishing process, let's explore why KDP stands out as one of the most popular platforms for self-publishing authors.

1. **Passive Income Opportunities**
   KDP provides an incredible opportunity for generating passive income. After uploading

your ebook and setting a price, it will be available for sale on Amazon around the clock. Every time a reader purchases your book, you earn royalties. Over time, as you expand your catalog, your earnings can grow steadily with minimal ongoing effort.

2. **Global Reach**
   One of the most appealing benefits of KDP is its ability to connect you with a global audience. Your ebook will be available on Amazon's marketplaces in over 100 countries, giving you access to readers in regions you may never have reached with traditional publishing. This global presence increases your potential to make an impact and sell books to people from all walks of life.

3. **Complete Control and Flexibility**
   With KDP, you maintain complete control over your ebook. From pricing and content to design and marketing, you're free to make decisions that align with your vision. You can update your book at any time, adjust pricing as needed, and experiment with various marketing strategies. This flexibility empowers you to take charge of your success.

4. **Easy Setup with Low Costs**
   Getting started on KDP is straightforward,

and the platform is free to use. You won't have to worry about expensive upfront costs, such as printing or distribution fees. Amazon only takes a small commission on each sale, making it a great option for beginner authors who want to test the waters of ebook publishing without financial risk.

Steps to Success with KDP

Now that you understand the advantages of publishing on KDP, let's take you through the essential steps to get your ebook live on Amazon.

Step 1: Writing and Formatting Your Ebook

1. **Writing Your Ebook**
   Your first priority is writing a high-quality ebook. Whether you're crafting a non-fiction guide, a novel, or a collection of short stories, it's essential to produce content that resonates with your target audience. Keep these key points in mind while writing:

   - **Know Your Audience:** Tailor your writing to meet the needs, interests, and expectations of your readers.

- **Consistency is Key:** Develop a writing routine to stay on track, especially if you're working on a longer project.

- **Edit and Proofread:** After finishing your draft, thoroughly edit your ebook to ensure it's polished and error-free. Consider hiring a professional editor for a final review.

2. **Formatting Your Ebook**

   Once your ebook is written, it needs to be formatted for a seamless reading experience. Proper formatting ensures that your book displays well across all devices, including Kindles, smartphones, and tablets. Here's what to keep in mind:

   - **File Format:** KDP accepts formats like .doc, .docx, ePub, and PDF, but the best format for Kindle is .mobi, which you can create using Amazon's Kindle Create tool.

   - **Page Layout:** Use a simple, readable font (like Times New Roman or Arial) and ensure there's adequate white space around the text.

- **Table of Contents:** Include a clickable table of contents to help readers navigate your book.

- **Images:** If your ebook includes images, make sure they are high-quality and properly sized.

- **Margins and Spacing:** Keep margins and spacing consistent throughout for a clean, professional look. You can use tools like Microsoft Word, Scrivener, or Calibre to help format your ebook easily.

Step 2: Creating Your KDP Account

If you don't already have an Amazon account, you'll need to create one to publish your ebook on KDP. Here's how to get started:

- Go to the KDP website and sign up using your Amazon credentials or create a new account.

- Fill in the required tax and payment details so Amazon can process your earnings. Once your account is set up, you're ready to upload your ebook.

Step 3: Uploading Your Ebook to KDP

Uploading your ebook to KDP is a simple process. Follow these steps:

- **Log In to KDP:** Once your account is ready, log in to the KDP dashboard.

- **Create a New Title:** Click the "+ Kindle eBook" button to start a new project.

- **Enter Your Book Details:** Provide essential information such as your ebook's title, author name, and description. Be specific with keywords and categories to ensure your book is easy to find.

- **Upload Your Manuscript:** Click "Upload eBook Manuscript" to submit your formatted file.

- **Design a Cover:** If you don't have a cover, use KDP's Kindle Cover Creator to design one, or upload your own.

- **Set Pricing and Royalties:** Choose your ebook's price and royalty rate (35% or 70%). For the 70% royalty option, your ebook must be priced between $2.99 and $9.99. Once everything is set, click "Publish," and your ebook will be live within 24 to 48 hours.

Step 4: Marketing Your Ebook

While publishing is a huge milestone, marketing is what drives sales. Here are some strategies to promote your ebook:

- **Use Social Media:** Share your ebook's launch and progress on platforms like Instagram, Twitter, and Facebook. Engage with your audience by posting excerpts or running special promotions.

- **Build an Email List:** Offer incentives like a free chapter or a discount to encourage people to join your email list. Use this list to notify potential readers about your ebook's release or upcoming promotions.

- **Run Amazon Ads:** Consider using Amazon's advertising platform to run targeted ads for your ebook, boosting its visibility.

- **Encourage Reviews:** Ask readers to leave reviews, which play a significant role in how your ebook ranks on Amazon. Positive reviews increase the chances of attracting new readers.

Key Takeaways

Publishing your ebook through Kindle Direct Publishing is a powerful way to share your expertise and earn passive income. By writing and formatting your ebook, uploading it to KDP, and promoting it effectively, you can launch a successful ebook business. Remember, achieving success in ebook publishing requires patience, persistence, and strategic marketing. But with the right approach, you can build a lasting presence that generates income for years to come. Stay dedicated to your goals and watch your ebook business thrive!

Conclusion

You've now explored various side hustles that can help boost your income. Each opportunity brings its own unique challenges and rewards, but the secret to success lies in taking action. The first step is to choose a side hustle that aligns with your skills, interests, and the time you can realistically commit. Be honest with yourself about what you can manage while maintaining balance in your life.

Take Action Today

The most crucial step you can take right now is to choose the side hustle that excites you the most. Don't wait for everything to be perfect—just get started. The longer you wait, the longer it will take to see results. Even if you're not 100% sure about the path, the best way to find your way is to jump in and learn through doing. Starting small is key. There's no need to go all-in at the beginning; take manageable steps, learn from each phase, and refine your approach as you go. The more you do, the clearer the path will become.

Choose the Right Side Hustle for Your Skills and Time

It's essential to pick a side hustle that fits your current skill set and the amount of time you can realistically dedicate. Whether you prefer something that requires minimal startup or are willing to invest more time upfront for long-term results, choosing the right fit will help keep you motivated and on track.

Keep in mind that a side hustle is meant to enhance your life—not overwhelm it. It should provide extra income, foster personal growth, and give you a sense of fulfillment.

Start Small, Learn, and Grow Consistently

Consistency is your greatest ally on this journey. Start with small, manageable goals and build on them as you gain more experience. Track your progress, celebrate your wins, and learn from any setbacks. The growth you see in your side hustle will mirror your growth as a person.

The journey may have its ups and downs, but with perseverance and a mindset focused on learning, you can transform your side hustle into a profitable and fulfilling venture. Keep moving forward, stay committed, and embrace the growth process. Your side hustle success is within reach.

www.ingramcontent.com/pod-product-compliance
Lightning Source LLC
Chambersburg PA
CBHW071055240526
45469CB00006BD/2315